A PICTURE OF ME

The Lyrical Poetry
of a
Texas Minstrel

C. D. COLLINS

DEDICATION

This book is dedicated to all my North Garland High School English teachers; Mrs. Lowrance, Mrs. Hunt, and Mrs. Parrot. Mrs. Barbara Parrot was my English Literature teacher my senior year in high school. She took our class to see plays such as "Man of La Mancha" as well as Hal Holbrook's one-man play of Mark Twain. I had an interest in reading books ever since I was small, but Mrs. Parrott sparked the interest in plays and other forms of writing.

C.D. Collins

FOREWARD

I have a unique relationship to the material contained within these pages. Most of the poems found in this book are actually songs, and I've had the privilege to hear them with music and melody attached. I also had the privilege to grow up listening to them. My father had a vast repertoire of songs he would play and sing, and his catalog consisted of both songs by other artists and his originals. I was so used to my Dad's songs that I did not realize he had written them until I was much older. Song like "Shadows," "Sky," and "Picture of Me" were mainstays of my childhood, and I thought then, and still think now, that they hold their own with other songs of the era.

I grew up to write my own songs, and on the few occasions when I have encouraged others to write songs, they almost always respond by saying, "I can't do that." I never felt this way. To me, writing songs was just something people did, like using forks, or riding bikes, or wearing hats. It never occurred to me that writing was difficult, or that I might not be any good at it, and for fostering an environment where creativity was a part of everyday life, I will always be infinitely grateful to my father.

My biggest fear is that the quality of the songs will not come through on the page. Songs are different than poems. Poems posses a self-contained rhythm, a sort of map that tells you how to read and interpret the piece. The music and melody dictate the rhythm in a song, and when the lyrics exist apart from the music, they often lose their effect. Lines and phrases that sound poignant and powerful when sung, fall flat when read.

So I ask you to remember that while lyrically complete, most of these songs lack an essential component. But even without their music, I promise you they still hold the power and promise that spoke to me when I was young. "Shadows," "Without You," "Picture of Me," "Summer Rain-" these songs still resonate for me as much today as they did twenty years ago. Later works that appear in this collection contain more heartbreak, desperation, and bitterness than the earlier poems, but hope still shines through even the darkest verses. Nowhere is this more apparent than in the gut-wrenching "Faith: Shaken not Stirred," a heartbreaking examination of a man having an existential crisis during a harrowing ordeal.

I think we are all searching for something, and more than anything, I feel this slim volume gives a brief glimpse into the life of a man that is always searching, always questioning, and always trying to make himself better. I hope you find something in these pages that reverberates with you, something to think about when the night gets long and there is no one to keep you company but your thoughts.

Sean Collins
2018

CONTENTS

ACKNOWLEDGMENTS

I would like to thank my son, Sean D. Collins, for his hard work editing this collection of lyrical poetry. While at times I may have overridden some of his editing suggestions, those instances were few. He is far more educated than I am, and a literary genius. His work on this means so much.

I would also like to thank my daughter, Kasey Shea Collins, who is also far more educated than I am. She is a high school teacher, mother of my grandson, Tristan, and all around goddess. Her support also means the world to me.

Thank you, also, to my parents, Dan and Juanita Collins, who have always provided me much love and support, and who taught me most of the values that I hold dear.

Finally, I would like to thank my wonderful wife, Leslie, who endeavored night and day to put this collection together. Without her this little book would have never been possible. She always seems to have more faith in me than I deserve, and much more than I have in myself.

1 WESTERN

It seems that people are always trying to put everything into categories. They place people, animals, places, and things into categories, thinking it will help them understand things better, but it does not. Some things just defy categorization. Texas is one of those places. It seems that some would divide our country into different areas, such as the Northeast, South (which is really the Southeast, to categorize it- see what I did there?), Southwest, Northwest and Midwest. However, Texas does not fit into any of those categories. Texas is, well, Texas.

Texas is a place unlike any other. The culture is different. The people are different. Its landscape ranges from the tall pine forests of East Texas, to the high desert of the Big Bend. It stretches from the Plains in the northwest and then east to the black land prairie of north central Texas. There is the Texas Hill Country in the central part of the state and the 370 or so miles of Texas coastline (as the crow flies).

Texas is known for its cowboys, Native Americans, Tejanos, its high tech industries, and do not forget the oil and gas industry, which is my former area of expertise. There is fishing, farming, and a host of other industries.

The people of Texas are very independent, don't ask for much, and make do with what they have, while always trying to be better.

There is great variety in the food, from Tex-Mex, to seafood, to Bar-Be-Que, to just good old cowboy fare. Beef is king in Texas. If you do not enjoy eating in Texas, then you do not like food.

The point of all this is that Texas is Different. It is in a category of its own. God Bless Texas!

TEXAS
(2016)

I left my home on Sunday, dreading the coming Monday,
The long road ahead was hard to see.
And I know that Monday will only see me halfway
To that old home place where I want to be

'Cause you see I tried hard, not to do wrong,
But the city life was not for me,
And I know I have to get back to where I belong.
My life's in Texas, not in Tennessee.

Well the songs I've been singing, didn't come close to bringing
The success I hoped would come to me.
And I can't help thinking, that maybe all that drinking
Has slowing been killing me.

It's lonesome when you don't belong, singing your lonesome songs
At bars and dives all across Dixie.
I knew it wouldn't be long, before I packed up all my songs
And took my old guitar back home to stay.

I'm going back to Texas, that's where I belong,
Where the sky is big and the lonesome road is free.
Going back to Texas, singing a Texas song.
Texas is the only place I want to be.

And now that big ol' Texas sky is twinkling over me
And that Texas moon seems even brighter now, you see.
The Texas bars are just like a long lost friend calling me.
That's why Texas is my home, not Tennessee.

Yes I'm back in Texas, that's where I belong,
Where the sky is big and the sunshine makes my day.
Yes I'm back in Texas, singing a Texas song.
Texas is the place I'm gonna stay.

8 SECONDS

(2016)

Eight seconds, that's all I need.
Eight Seconds, how long can that be?
A very long time it seems to me.
Long enough for me to see
My whole life flash in front of me.
Eight seconds, a few blinks of an eye.
Long enough for me to wonder why,
Long enough to almost learn to fly,
Long enough to hear my own cries.
Long enough to wonder if I'll live or die.
Eight seconds, what did I think I'd gain?
Eight seconds, could it be worth all the pain?
Eight seconds, why couldn't I refrain
From riding here in the mud and the rain?
Will I ever be able to ride again?
Eight seconds, it's over and I still live.
I gave all I had, nothing left to give.
I feel like my body has been run through a sieve.
That bull is not one I'll soon forgive,
But the thrill of the ride I'll never outlive.

Way back in the mid 1970's when I was in college at Stephen F. Austin State University, some of my drunken cowboy friends who were in the Rodeo Club convinced me that I needed to ride a bull. Being stubborn, over confident and a little inebriated, I gave it a shot. I figured out that the hard part about riding a bull isn't staying on, but trying to get off without killing yourself. From this experience comes this poem.

PECAN PIE
(2014)

Pecan pie, pecan pie
Just can't get enough of that pecan pie.
You can say pe-kahn or you can say pee-can,
Doesn't matter on which side you stand.
But that Pecan pie, pecan pie
Just can't get enough of that pecan pie.
Because pecan pie, pecan pie,
Ain't nothing better than pecan pie.

Most people eat them at Thanksgiving,
And at Christmas is another time.
During the Christmas season
They are enjoyed with a good wine.
Up north in Lamar County
Old Joe's pecan orchard lies.
Some three thousand pecan trees
Grow under the blue Texas sky.

And every late November,
As leaves begin to fall,
Joe rolls out his old Shaker,
And shakes trees short and tall.
The pecans fall to the ground.
Joe scoops them up and then
He and Jerry are finally ready
For the harvesting to begin

Fresh pecans from Joe's orchard,
Harvested by all his friends,
Sorted by the hands of neighbors.
Sorted again and again.
Nine super sacks sorted on Saturday
And I can almost taste that pecan pie.
My old knees hurt from all the work,
It's a wonder I don't die.

Pecan pie, pecan pie,
Just can't get enough of that pecan pie.
You can say pe-kahn or you can say pee-can,
Doesn't matter on which side you stand.
But that Pecan pie, pecan pie,
Just can't get enough of that pecan pie.
Because pecan pie, pecan pie,
Ain't nothing better than pecan pie.

You might ask why I tell this story
And I tell you that this ain't no lie,
That my mama she does make
The very best pecan pie.
And there's only one thing in the world better
Than pecan pie, and that I know,
And that would be having
A great friend like my friend Joe.

Pecan pie, pecan pie,
Just can't get enough of that pecan pie.
You can say pe-kahn or you can say pee-can
Doesn't matter on which side you stand.
But that Pecan pie, pecan pie,
Just can't get enough of that pecan pie.
Because pecan pie, pecan pie,
Ain't nothing better than pecan pie.

I wrote this for my friend, Joe Jeter. I have known Joe since I was about 4 years old. He owns a pecan orchard and farm in Texas. Joe is as good of guy as you are ever going to find. He has been taking my Mom and Dad some pecans each year at harvest time. Sometimes, my Mom will make him a pecan pie. There isn't anything better. You pronounce it "pee- kahn" not "pee-can." A pee-can is something you go to the bathroom in.

TERLINGUA DESERT
(2016)

You see a stream
And I see an ocean.
You see a storm cloud
While I see a rainbow.
You see the hardships
Of life all around.
I see the mystery
Of life that abounds.

The western sun sets
Over Terlingua tonight.
The cinnabar shines red
In the cool desert night.
The night comes quickly
In the southwestern desert.
The wind stirs silently
In the soft desert light.

I'm up before dawn
On the morrow.
Up though the Chisos
My next camp to make.
My horse and my saddle
Are all I have with me.
My pony is steady
And knows the right trail to take.

And you're all caught up
In the buzz of the city.
Bright lights and crowds
Are home to you now.
And I am at home here
In the high lonesome desert.
I ride on with my horse and my saddle,
The sweat on my brow.

Sometimes I wonder
Where did it all go wrong?
Our paths seemed to cross
Then they forked left and right.
And sometimes I wonder
Do you ever think of me?
I think of you now
As I bed down for the night.

The high Texas desert
Is soft and it's lonesome.
The day's heat gives way
To the cool desert night.
The life of a drifter
Is not what you've chosen.
You chose the big city
And I chose the big sky.

The life of a drifter
It's quiet and it's lonely.
The city is busy
So crowded and loud.
You chose the city
And I chose the big sky.
I wonder who's wrong
And who might be right.

KRIS IS NOT A KRINGLE

There is a Kris that I have heard of,
And I have seen him a time or two.
No, he is not the Kris of Christmas,
And he won't bring presents to you.

Though his last name is not Kringle,
He's given us gifts, just the same.
Not the kind with wrapping paper,
A bow, or a label for your name.

No, this Kris is a legendary songwriter,
Songs that reach deep into your mind.
A new age prophet and a poet of sorts,
There are not very many of his kind.

His songs sing the music of our lives,
They echo from hills and beyond.
The songs filter down to the valley
To bring life to your own personal song.

So, please lift a glass and rejoice
To the Kris of the songwriting kind.
Just kick back, drink, and listen close
To his songs which are truly fine.

Note: If you don't know who the Kris I am referring to is, you are reading the wrong book.

BANK OF A RIVER

(2016)

All Hallows Eve, sitting by the bank of a river in Graham, Texas.
A little ways away some ducks and geese are causing a racket.
There are two Mallards, drake and a hen, a wood duck,
And several indeterminate types of ducks and geese
Honking and quacking through the lunch time.
They quiet down as the church bell rings the noon hour.
The little park by the river is almost deserted,
Sad for such a beautiful place.
A good place for meditation and reflection.
Cool autumn air rustling leaves just beginning to turn color;
Green to yellow, yellow to brown, not quite ready to fall.
A little gray squirrel teases the ducks and geese,
Darting in and out amongst them
Then quickly scampering up an old oak tree.
The ducks quack at him while the geese give chase,
Honking like an old Model T.
The gnarled, old oak tree in front of me seems to have a face in its bark,
An old man, Old Man Oak, looking out over the river, trees, and animals,
Keeping a quiet watch over the peaceful scene, vigilant in his task.
I believe I can see the trace of a smile in the old oak's face
As the ducks and geese quiet down and the squirrel climbs his limbs.
Perhaps all is as it should be on All Hallows Eve,
On the bank of a river in Graham, Texas.

EL YANKEE FANTASTICO

(2006)

Left Laredo this morning at half past ten.
Don't know exactly where I'm going, don't care where I've been.
Think I started out towards Corpus and Nueces Bay,
But now I think I'll head down South Padre way.

Bonnie Prince Billy playing on my radio.
He's stuck in Palm Beach with sand between his toes.
We wandering cowboys got so much to give.
I just don't understand how the other half lives.

Radiator's boiling; guess I better make a stop.
Ol' Texas sun's beating down making the pickup truck hot.
But I'll down a brew or two and I'll soon be ok,
And head back out down South Padre way.

With one boot In Texas,
One in Mexico,
Life moves so fast
But I'm taking things slow.
I don't know nothin'
But there's nothing to know,
That's why they call me
El Yankee Fantastico.

Thinking about the pretty senorita I left behind.
I just can't seem to get her off my mind.
Her flashing smile, the mischievous eyes,
But she quickly learned to see through my disguise.

Life is so hard for this music man,
Always moving town-to-town, playing one night stands.
Never stay in one place, never had a home,
Guess this ol' boy was always meant to roam.

With one girl in Texas,
One in Mexico,
I love the women
Where ever I go.
I'm a guitar gunslinger,
Yeah everybody knows
That's why they call me
El Yankee Fantastico.

Well adios, muchachos, it's time to leave,
With four bits in my pocket and nothin' up my sleeve.
Heading out to face another one night stand,
Playing country music with my rock and roll band.

With one gig in Texas,
One in Mexico,
Playing good music
Where ever we go.
With no pretensions
But with Texas soul,
That's why they call me
El Yankee Fantastico.

With my soul in Texas,
Heart in Mexico,
Playing good music
Where ever we go.
With no pretensions
But with Texas soul,
That's why they call me
El Yankee Fantastico.

GUITAR

(1994)

This guitar is old, but the music is bold,
Its character comes through
With each note and chord.

When it was young, and the strings barely strung,
Its top end was tinny
And bottom end was light.

But it improved with age, like the wisdom of a sage,
It's top end bright
And it's bottom end bold.

'Cause when it sings, and all its strings ring,
It's a song of soul
Built of love and toil.

When I pass on, I'll pass it along
To my son,
And when he's done,

He'll pass it along, so the music lives on
And brightens the day
Of those that pass it's way.

GUY, RUSTY, TOWNES AND ME

Roaming the Texas Highways,
All the dirt roads and country lanes,
The view never ceases to amaze me,
It's so good to be in Texas again.

I'm headed down to the Texas coast,
Rockport, Portland then Corpus Christi.
I am hoping to do a little fishing
And some sailing sounds right to me.

I have a love affair with Texas,
It's where my heart will always be
My old Martin guitar is traveling
With Guy, Rusty, Townes and me.

Their songs are always with me,
I hear them on the Texas breeze.
But at times, I get a hankering for
Some Jerry Jeff and Michael Murphy.

I see some ships coming in
To dock in Corpus Christi Bay.
To the west the setting sun
Signals the end to a Texas day.

I have a love affair with Texas,
It's where my heart will always be
My old Martin guitar is traveling
With Guy, Rusty, Townes and me.

Note: I know that Jerry Jeff Walker is not from Texas, but bless his heart, he got here just as quick as he could. Guy Clark, Townes Van Zandt, Rusty Wier and Michael Murphy were all fortunate enough to be born in the great State of Texas.

SHADE OF A LIVE OAK
(2016)

In the shade of an old live oak on the banks of the Pedernales
He sits and casts his troubles into the waters flowing by.
He thinks on the days when the Comanche rode through here
And he longs for the days of the past under the blue Texas sky.

The Comanche are gone now, along with the buffalo,
And all the wild horses are now up Wyoming way.
There is not much western left in the west now,
No longhorns in the brush like there were back in the day.

It brings a sigh to the sad, lonesome ole cowboy
In the shade of a live oak on the banks of the Pedernales today.
The Comanche, wild horses, the buff and rank longhorns
Are just memories that we seem to have lost along the way.

PINEY WOODS HIPPIE
(2016)

He looks like an old hippie, still wearing bell bottomed jeans,
Worn old hiking boots, and a floppy old hat,
He has years' worth of gray, grizzled whiskers but young youthful eyes,
And a forever smile on his craggy old face.
Just a small house in the pine trees, deep in east Texas,
Nine miles outside Nacogdoches, though it seems a hundred or more.
He chops firewood to sell to the town folk for winter,
Cut from the oaks interspersed with loblolly pine.
There are chickens he keeps for the eggs,
A couple of old barn cats to help keep the mice at bay,
And about an acre of beans, squash, onions, and cabbage,
All to eat or sell at the market in town.
He has an old guitar he plays at night time on the old porch.
Just an old flat top Martin played finger pick style.
He sings up some Beatles, some Nitty Gritty Dirt Band,
But the last one is always an old Rusty Weir song.
(Ah! The Fabulous Filler Brothers!)
He thinks back to college days at Stephen F. Austin,
Back when there were streakers and protesters and the girls burned
their bras.
Everyone was a philosophy major and a ninth semester freshman.
School was a way of life rather than an educational plan.
Everyone planned to be a thinker or a poet,
most ended up working a job for the man.
But he stayed true to the simple life in the piney woods
Not rich but his own man.
The old hippie feeds the chickens and talks to the cats, then goes
Back to the cabin, picks up the old guitar and gives it a quick tune.
He thinks for a moment then begins to pick the old guitar
Then an old Rusty Wier song he gently begins to croon.

SOUTHWEST TEXAS DESERT
(2017)

Well, the temperature must be a hundred and ten and that's for sure,
And I ain't seen any shade round here in at least two days or more.
The sun is so damn hot cactus cries out for a little water, if you please.
Blue Sky answers with cloudless eyes, can't get what you want, or what you need.
Southwest Texas ain't for the weak, whiners and posers won't last long.
You grow up here; you grow up crusty, willful, strong, and hard.
My jeans are old and faded from the hot Texas sun beating me so down.
My boots are old and ragged, worn clear down to the scorching Texas ground.
Life in the desert is hard, uncompromising, no guarantee of success or getting by.
Now I'm bedded down for the night by a campfire, staring up into the starlit sky.
It's a life that is hard, fraught with dangers and tribulations that come each day.
Yeah, life in the desert is harsh, but I wouldn't have it any other way.

TWINKLE IN THEIR EYE

(1980)

Many search for the secrets
Of oil beneath the ground.
But only few have ever learned
Of the ways it can be found.

Seismic Ships sail the seas,
Big rigs dot the land,
Searching for that hidden treasure
That is the lifeblood of man.

But only a handful have the knack
Of finding this mysterious wealth.
And they will never convince the others
That it's found with knowledge not with stealth.

And what of the ones that know
And often get asked why?
They just answer with a smile
And a certain twinkle in their eye.

THE LEGEND OF BUNION JOE
(1981)

There was an old oil finder named Joe,
Who had a bunion on his big toe.
Bunion Joe swore
That when it got sore,
That it was time to drill a new hole.

He'd walk 'round and 'round 'till it got red
And his toe actually felt half dead.
Wherever it hurt worse,
That was where to drill first,
At least that's what Bunion Joe said.

One day his big toe did turn blue,
And Joe did not know what to do.
"I drill when it's red,"
Bunion Joe said,
"But what do I do when it's blue?"

Joe finally worked the problem out
And decided what the toe was about.
When the toe turns blue
I'll know what to do,
I'll go offshore and drill a step out.

The step out was a major find,
And Joe's son didn't really mind.
When in Joe's will
He left the son not the well,
But his toe that was one of a kind.

2 LOVE AND HEARTBREAK, TEXAS STYLE

Love is a tricky thing that plays with the souls of the people that are lucky enough, or unlucky enough, to fall under its spell. It can bring you immense joy, or terrible heartbreak. At times it can just leave you so flabbergasted and without a clue that you have no idea which way to turn, or what to do. It can bring you to the heights of euphoria or take you to the depths of depression. In the end, it is worth all of that. I think.

WITHOUT YOU
(1987)

I saw the moonlight on the street tonight,
The wind was stirring but the night was quiet.
Thought I saw you in the window there.
Took me back to times when you still cared,
And I'll get by, and I'll survive,
Without you, without you,
Without you.

I use to think those were the best of times,
We'd lose ourselves in talk and cheap port wine.
Whatever happened to the good old days?
Whatever happened to make us change our ways?
And I'll get by, and I'll survive,
Without you, without you,
Without you.

I never saw it coming,
It took me by surprise.
I guess our days were numbered,
The best days of our lives.

I guess love is just a fleeting thing,
Well it fled away from me.
I guess you are the only love,
These eyes will ever see.
And I'll get by, and I'll survive,
Without you, without you,
Without you.

I saw the moonlight on the street tonight,
The wind was stirring but the night was quiet.
Guess I was dreaming of you again,
I love you now as I loved you then.
And I'll get by, and I'll survive,
Without you, without you,

FAIRY FLIGHT
(2001)

Feeling lost, lost inside your love
And I don't know if I'll ever be found again.
This love, at such a cost,
Worth the pound of flesh and heartbreak I feel.

Beautiful, lovely girl in deep blue mist,
Can you carry me away on your fairy wings of light?
Dying, from the inside out,
And I don't know if I'll ever be sane again.

Mount your horse of flame,
Things will never be the same,
Into the starry night, I see my love take flight.
I know I will love you for all time.

Riding, in a fairy land of mist,
And your eyes are closed with every kiss.
Take flight, into a double moon sky.
The night's not dark enough to hide my love.

And love it seems,
Never comes without a fall.
But if you answer the call, make love yours,
You can ride into the sky, on the wings of love.

Mount your horse of flame,
Things will never be the same,
Into the starry night, I see my love take flight.
I know I will love you for all time.

BLUE AND BLACK AND GRAY
(2014)

Things been changing so fast I can't believe.
Sometimes I can't keep up with myself.
Life goes by so fast sometimes I can't see.
Can't help myself or anyone else.

And each time I get to feeling so self assured
Something always happens to bring me 'round.
Every time it seems it's finally getting easy
You always go and try to bring me down.

But I'm still here and I just won't go away.
I was here when you came along.
I'm still here and I'm not bound to change.
I'll be here long after you're gone.

Roses were red, way long before I ever knew
All about the different colors and hues.
I found the thorns that glisten with the dew,
And I found the thorns that came with you.

And every time those flowers begin to fade away,
I pick up a new paintbrush and start again.
I paint those roses, in blue, black, and gray,
And know they'll turn to red again, someday.

Yeah I'm still here, and I just won't go away,
And I've been here all along.
I'm just hanging on, living out each day,
Trying to find where I belong.

PRINCESS
(2000)

To experience your laugh,
To breathe in your smile.
Just to hold your hand,
If only for a while.

To share hopes and dreams,
To make plans and schemes.
Oh, my love I tell you.
This is the closest to Heaven I've been.

Just to have you love me,
Just to have you call.
Just to have your arms around me,
When my world starts to crumble and fall.

And I will Love you forever,
Love, you know you're the best part of me.
And I will hold you forever,
And keep you beside me for all eternity.

And on the day I die,
Before I'm laid to rest,
Take me and hold me,
My head against your breast.

And let a tear fall slowly,
From your cheek down to my face,
To bring me back to life again,
A life full of peace and of Grace.

And I will Love you forever,
Love, you know you're the best part of me.
And I will hold you forever,
And keep you beside me for all eternity.

WINGS OF TEARS
(1999)

Well I've never really run away,
But I've been waiting on a rainy day,
To come and wash my tears away.

And people seem to come and go,
Some moving fast, some moving slow.
But most never seem to get anyplace.

Dreams escape on wings of tears
Bled from bloodshot eyes.
Just what it is I have to fear
Should come as no surprise.

I use to want to roam the world
But now I just seek a place to stay,
Where I can be at peace.

Places change and people go
But all I ever really know,
Is how I seem to stay the same.

Dreams escape on wings of tears
Bled from bloodshot eyes.
Just what it is you have to fear
Should come as no surprise.

Fear can break your heart,
Drop you to your knees.
Fear can tear you apart,
Blind you so you cannot see.

Dreams escape on wings of tears
Bled from bloodshot eyes.
Just what it is we have to fear
Should come as no surprise.

I searched, I read, I thought about
Just what makes the world go 'round
And why we're really here.

And what it comes down to
Is not how much you've got, but what
You've given and been given in return.

Dreams exist on wings of angels
That dance before my eyes.
And that I have nothing to fear
Should come as no surprise.

Dreams exist on wings of angels
That dance before my eyes.
And that I have nothing to fear
Comes as no surprise.

DELIRIUM
(2000)

Maybe I should have known,
My mind would be blown,
Lost forever in your eyes.
Guess I was bound to fail.
Seems I never prevail,
It's so useless, I'm so lost.

And I'll never again see
Those stars shine in your eyes.
I'm a loser, I lost what I found.
I'm a loser, I've toppled my crown
And I don't think that I will ever
Come back to the ground.

I see stormy skies
When I look in your eyes.
All your pain, God, put it on me.
And I just can't explain,
How I seemed to have changed.
My soul is yours, gone forever.

And I'll never again feel
The warmth of you in my arms.
I'm a loser, I lost what I found.
I'm a loser, I've toppled my crown,
And I don't think that my heart
Will ever come 'round.

God, I know you're gone.
How did my heart go so wrong?
Love is such a game.
I lost, and I feel ashamed.

Help me, I need you.
I'm trapped inside these walls.
I guess I didn't know
The way things would go,

Fooled myself and lost my heart.
I never wanted to hold,
Never want to control
Just want to share, now torn apart.

And I'll never again feel
The passion that you bring,
I'm lonely, love has run away.
I feel so lost now,
I don't know what to say.
I love you; I'll never let that get away.

EARTHQUAKE
(2000)

I've been so lost now, I don't have you,
Since you left and went away.
I walk the empty streets at night
Dreaming I am by your side.
I see your face in the people I meet
And it's driving me so mad.
It hurts so, honey, I got to have you,
Because you're the best I ever had.

All along I knew it couldn't last,
This strange romance of ours.
An hour here and maybe two hours there,
Just not very much time to say,
All the things that I hold within my heart,
And all the things I have in mind.
And without that chance we just can't survive.
Oh, I let you slip away.

I've stumbled, I fell down,
I've got up and turned around.
I've struggled, and fought hard,
I've got high, I've been pushed down.
Been through it all,
Your memory remains,
Oh, God I just got to get back to you.
Just got to get back to you.

I've cried all day, and I cried all night.
Something is wrong, nothing is right,
And everything, keeps falling down.
My life crumbles and falls out of sight.
Oh! My love, I miss you,
I need you more than I can show.
And oh! Love, I want to kiss you,
You'll be my greatest love, I know.

Every hour that I sit and think of you,
You just get farther away.
And it's so hard I don't think I'll get through,
Oh, even one more day.
Cause all the things that I trust and hold so dear
Don't mean a thing without you.
And If I can't have you I think I just might die,
Alone here drowning in my tears.

I'M SO IN LOVE WITH YOU
(2000)

I'm sorry I never lived up to
All the expectations in you heart.
I'm sorry that I'm to blame
For so much that drove us apart.
I'm sorry for the things I've done
But I don't know what to do.
I'm so in love with you, I'm so in love with you.

I never meant to hurt you
Or to cause you any pain.
I would never desert you,
But we are apart all the same.
And ever time you change your mind
I just never know what to do.
I'm so in love with you, I'm so in love with you.

I never meant to love you,
But I couldn't help myself.
I never wanted to need you,
But you know just how I felt.
And every time I see your face
I realize what I had to lose.
I'm so in love with you, I'm so in love with you.

I never wanted to be alone,
But I find myself alone anyhow.
I never wanted to be apart,
But you're with someone new now.
And every time I think of you
I just don't know what to do.
I'm so in love with you, I'm so in love with you.

THE GIRL WITH THE BEAUTIFUL SMILE (for Kasey)
(1996)

Driving a fast car I came to a stop
As the light changed from green to red.
A young girl stopped and asked for a ride,
Said she was headed straight ahead.
So she got in and said to me,
"Let's just drive around awhile."
That's how I came to know
The girl with the beautiful smile.

We drove ahead for quite awhile
And I stole glances when I could.
I could see she was pretty, and had a beautiful smile,
That danced when she spoke a word.
Then we stopped to get a bite,
At a small and quiet café.
Again I fell in love with that beautiful smile,
On that soft, warm summer day.

She talked of problems with boyfriends she had,
I said it couldn't be that bad.
She said she was glad that I was there,
I was the only friend she had.
It was getting late and time to go,
So I headed off down the road.
That's when I realized how much I love,
That girl that I'd come to know.

We got home, and said good night,
As I tucked her into bed,
She looked up at me and said "Thank you Daddy,
It was a real good time I had."
So I kissed her 'night, and turned off the light,
Then went outside for awhile,
I really can't explain how much I love the girl
With the beautiful, dancing smile.

FOR THE LIFE OF ME
(1998)

For the life of me I can't figure
Out the thoughts hidden behind those eyes.
I'm feeling somewhat jaded
And I can't tell the truth from the lies.

All along I should have known
Just how you thought of me.
But I guess it didn't matter,
You were the only thing I could see.

I never, no never
Thought about the end.
I waited, anticipated,
But it only brought more pain.

And I guess I should know,
That my heart you'll never see.
But that you'd ever leave me,
I never thought it, for the life of me.

Don't know how it got so crazy.
Somehow people came between
My love for you and your heart.
It's not something I could have foreseen.

Do we go our separate ways,
Or can we try to work things out?
I'm feeling so lost now,
Got to let these feelings out.

I never, no never
Thought about the end.
I waited, anticipated,
But it only brought more pain.

And I guess I should know
That my heart you'll never see.
But that you'd ever leave me,
I never thought it, for the life of me.

HEART IN YOUR HANDS
(2000)

Oh! I've never been much with words, Love,
Or for expressing just how I feel.
Never learned to share my emotions,
Never learned to show what was real.

Every day I get so much older,
See my life fading away so fast.
And more and more now I wonder.
Have I done anything that will last?

Life's so confusing, fragile and amusing,
Memories lost on the wind.
And I'm still trying, and all the while dying,
Crying and choking on my own sin.

I've poured out my heart to you, Love,
And placed it gently into your hands.
In pieces my heart has been broken.
Scattered like blood in the sand.

I've been trying to find what is true, Love,
To determine the right from the wrong.
If only I'd known when I started
That this would all have taken so long.

And though much of my search has been futile,
I have found one undeniable truth.
That through pain and depression all my life long,
My heart and soul still belong to you.

Life's so confusing, fragile and amusing,
Memories lost on the wind.
And I'm still trying, and all the while dying,
Crying and choking on my own sin.

Most of my life I've been so wrong, Love,
While searching for truth in my soul.
And just who I am, is not who I seem,
And I know I've been playing the wrong role.

Now I know my stage is not of this world
Because nothing I've found here is real.
Though my spirit is broken, defeated I'm not,
Because my heart belongs to you still.

Life's so confusing, fragile and amusing,
Memories lost on the wind.
And I'm still trying, and all the while dying,
Crying and choking on my own sin.

I've poured out my heart to you, Love,
And placed it gently into your hands.
In pieces my heart has been broken,
Scattered like blood in the sand.
Scattered like blood in the sand.

STARS IN YOUR EYES

(2000)

Well, I know I'm to blame.
I have caused all your pain.
I'm so sorry.
I know I have been told,
Take my hand now and fold.
I'm not bluffing
And I can't see the sky
For the stars in your eyes.

I'm so lost now,
Too lost to be found.
It's such a cost now,
But not in dollars or pounds.
But I love you,
My feet don't touch the ground
And I don't care
If I ever come around.

It's more than a game,
And nothing is ever the same.
All the pictures of you
I see at night,
With your eyes shining bright,
And never dimming.
I can't feel the knife,
For the love in my heart.

Because I'm lost now,
So lost in you.
Such a cost now,
I don't know what to do.
But I love you,
Please don't say we are through.
I don't care as long
As you let me hang around.

Because I'm lost now,
Love is really strange.
Such a cost,
I feel I'm deranged.
But I love you,
God knows that it's true.
I don't ever want to be
Where you're not in my life.

I know I've been told,
That I come on too bold,
But I love you.
And I know that it's strange,
This silly old game,
But it's your turn now.
I can't stop because I feel
You're the one that God meant for me.

Because I'm lost now,
Love is really strange.
Such a cost,
I don't know what to do.
But I love you,
Please don't say we are through.
I don't care as long
As you will let me hang around.

HEART OF STONE

(1998)

If your heart of stone
Should weather, then
Crumble and turn fine,
Be washed to the sea
And disappear into
The shifting sands of time.

Then I'll slowly watch
Those sands sift through
These hands of mine.
Just looking for a grain
Of hope with eyes
That are completely blind.

Though your Irish eyes
Are smiling, the look
They send is cold.
Green daggers penetrate
Deep down to the
Very depths of my troubled soul.

Confusion often erupts,
And all these feelings
Just make me feel so old.
Mystery of life,
Thy name is woman,
Or that's what I've been told.

Stuck here in a season
Without any wind,
You've taken it from my sails.
I sit becalmed,
Waiting for fresh air
To come again in the morning's mail.

Everything that's been
Said before will be
Said again, without fail.
Turn me away,
Turn me out today,
For my coffin another cruel nail.

But there comes a time
In soft summer days,
Sipping rose red wine,
When I think of ways
And simpler days,
Back to a time when you were mine.

You win, you lose,
Based on what you do,
Happens every time.
I'll not regret
A day with you,
I'll toast you one more time.

SLIPPING THROUGH MY FINGERS
(1985)

It slipped through my fingers,
But what could I do?
I tried to hold on
But it slipped right on through.

Pictures on my ceiling,
Mirrors on my wall,
I tried to hold on
But it did not hear my call.

'Round and 'round we went,
Down on the sand by the sea.
Knowing it was gone
Was pure hell for me.

And how do I answer,
My pleading, bleeding heart?
How was I to know,
That we would have to part?

Out on my own now,
So lost and depressed,
Searching for love,
An embrace, a caress.

This path I will follow,
Wherever it may lead.
Wondering where love is,
And who can she be?

Slipping through my fingers,
Like sand falling from my hand.
Slipping through my fingers,
Why, I don't understand.

Just slipping through my fingers,
Oh I wish you were mine.
Just slipping through my fingers,
Like I'm slipping through time.

WITH MY TEARS

(2002)

Have I told you how I feel?
Have I told you love is real?
Have I told you
Love's just a step away?

Have I told you that I cry,
Nights without you by my side?
Without you,
I just can't make one more day.

Have I told you how it feels,
To be without you and all alone?
Have I told you how it feels,
To be soaked through to the bone,
With my tears?

And all the nights I cried,
With all the breaths I've sighed,
I just can't
Get you off my mind.

And with all the things I've done,
The battles lost and won.
I don't think,
A greater love I'll ever find.

Have I told you how it feels,
To be without you and all alone?
Have I told you how it feels,
To be soaked through to the bone,
With my tears?

Now this story has been told,
And my words have been quite bold,
So no doubt
Should be left inside your heart.

Now you know just how I feel,
You know my love is real.
I can't survive,
If we remain apart.

And I've told you how it feels,
To be without you and all alone.
And I've told you how it feels,
To be soaked through to the bone,
With my tears.

LOVES'S SONG
(Broken Promise)
(1996)

Summer comes, and slowly slips away.
I'm left dreaming of those bright summer days.
But winter comes to us all,
Cold wind slicing through to our hearts.
But you don't have to despair
With love in your heart.

I remember when I loved the first time,
Kisses as sweet as elderberry wine.
True love will last forever,
And true love never falls apart.
And the love I found the first time
Is still a love of my heart.

Rainbow across a new blue sky,
And my love so strong it will never die.
Love was meant to last forever,
Love was never meant to end.
I gave my love away forever,
What a long great love it's been.

3 SPIRITUAL

I have been involved in Church most of my life. From a little boy, crawling under the pews at Freeman Heights Baptist Church in Garland, Texas with my best friend Richard Todd, to other churches such as First Baptist Church in Garland, and churches in places like Gillette, Wyoming and Ada, Oklahoma, Church was a big part of my life. I arrived back in Garland, and back at Freeman Heights, where I was involved playing guitar, and sometimes bass, in the church on Sundays, finally becoming the Contemporary Service Praise Leader, and led the music for the youth group at night.

IF YOU SEE ME FALL

(1987)

If you see me fall,
Stumble a time or two,
Don't worry, don't worry,
I'll be fine soon.

If you see me cry,
Tear falling down my face,
Don't worry, don't worry,
I'm in God's grace.

There's a world out there
Where people just don't care,
But I will be all right.
I have God's love,
He's always by my side
And I'll be all right.

So if you hold my hand,
Walk with me for awhile,
I can tell you, I can tell you,
As I look into your smile.

We live in a time of grace,
Paid for by God's only Son.
It can be yours, And we'll be there,
When His Kingdom comes.

There's a world out there
Where people just don't care,
But I will be all right.
I have God's love,
He's always by my side
And I'll be all right.

So if you see me fall,
Stumble a time or two,
Don't worry, don't worry
I'll be fine soon.

I'M COMING HOME
(1998)

I walked the road when I was young, from the dawn to the setting sun
From Paradise to Hollywood, I walked a road less understood,
And now, I'm coming home

I walked a road less traveled, stayed to the right instead of wrong
And though many times I've stumbled, You were there to help me
along, and now, I'm coming home

I turned to you in conflict, I turned to You and pain
You were the warmth in my winters, and in the summer You were my
rain, and now, I'm coming home

I'm coming home to where the heart is, home to where the love is,
Home to where You hold for me a place.
I'm coming home to where the light shines, home to where the heart
shines,
Home to where I can finally see Your face.
I'm coming home, I'm coming home, and Lord, I'm coming home.

Though I leave many loves behind, not for one minute do I mind.
I've tried to do what You asked me to, now I know it's time to be with
You, and now, I'm coming home

I ask that You watch over those, we could never quite reach.
And I pray that you send someone, that of Your love and grace can
preach, but now, I'm coming home

I'm coming home to where the heart is, home to where the love is,
Home to where You hold for me a place.
I'm going home to where the light shines, home to where the heart
shines,
Home to where I can finally see Your face.
I'm coming home, I'm coming home, and Lord, I'm coming home.

LITTLE ANGEL
(2002)

I've been wasting too much time
Trying to ease this troubled mind.
When I'm in my hiding place,
I'm alone and seek your face.

Little angel come to me.
Lift me up and set me free.
Spread your wings and help me fly,
'Cause pretty soon I'm gonna die.

Little angel spread your wings.
Come and fly over me.
Fly on through the sky.
Angel teach me to fly.

Like a vision in the night
Help my love to take flight.
Lift me high above this life,
Pull me out of all my strife.

Fly on high over me.
Lift me up so I can see
The light ahead and life behind,
Pretty soon we're gonna shine.

Little angel help me see
All that this love can be.
I can't find it on my own,
Little angel take me home.

IDENTITY CRISIS
(1997)

There are times when I want to be noticed,
And times when I want no one to know my name.
There are times when I seek anonymity
To help me escape all the blame.
I want to be known, and then I don't.
I'm hiding out in an old overcoat.
I want to yell out my name
And not be afraid to accept the blame.
I want to meet people and have fun.
I want to go where the prize is won.
I want to be by myself,
And I want to be someone else.

So, please give me a handle,
Someone give me a line.
Someone please help me find
A name that is mine.
Help me open up,
Open up to myself.
Help me to shed
These scars I've worn.
Please help me to
Be reborn.
Help me to change
And find the man I need to be.

I'm tired of fighting these wars,
Battles, and games all by myself.
Find me someone to lean on,
Help me to take my life down off the shelf.
Take my money, I don't mind.
Seems I'm always working overtime.
Trying to get ahead,
But I know I'll only wind up dead.
I want to have fun, feel the sun
And dance until the night is done.
Then I want to go out the door
And lie in the arms of the Lord.

LORD I FEEL SO ALONE
(1999)

Lord, I feel so alone tonight.
Lord, pick me up and take me to the light.
My hands are shaking,
My body is aching.
Lord, let me put my hope in You.

Lord, I feel so frightened.
I don't want to wake up and face another day.
My heart is broken,
But Your word is spoken.
Lord, stand with me I pray.

The night comes, darkness touches my soul.
Lord I give it up to You to take control.
It's all too much,
I need Your touch,
Lord, hear me, I pray.

Lord, help make it through one more day.

COME HERE AGAIN
(2000)

I feel I've been bruised and left for dead.
I feel the wound is all in my head.
Down here they don't even know my name.
Life here is nothing but a silly game.
Where are You going, where have You been,
Do You think You'll ever come here again?

I see, my friend, You've been through the wars.
I see the blood stained wounds and Your scars.
Nail scars, still seen plainly on Your hands.
I know You were so much more than just a man.
Where did You go, where have You been,
Do You think You'll ever come here again?

Blood is dripping, from Your furrowed and scarred brow.
Do You know where You are going to now?
I fear Hell now, worse is yet to come.
Do I stay or do I turn and run?
Where did You go, where have You been,
Do you think You'll come here again?

DEMONS

(1990)

The candle flame flickers
As the wind blows through the room.
My heartbeat is a hollow echo,
Like the echo from a tomb.

The light casts flickering shadows,
Dancing demons on the wall.
Are they here to comfort me
Or will they end it all?

Will they carry me away silently
Into the gloom of night?
Or will I not go willingly
And put up a heroic fight?

Oh! The demons of the candlelight
Bow their heads to the fading fire.
They know I will not follow them,
I answer to a higher power.

For I know that my demons
Are products of myself.
Greed, hate, and hunger
Are the demons that steal my wealth.

For I cannot be harmed at all
By dancing demons on the wall.
But hate, bigotry, and poverty
May one day consume us all.

Oh! The demons of the candlelight
Bow their heads to the fading fire.
They know I will not follow them,
I answer to a higher power.

THE THIEF
(1990)

The thief comes walking down the road of life.
He takes away our innocence, steals the shine from our eyes.
The thief comes strolling
And the people say, "I don't care."
And the thief just keeps on rolling,
And there ain't anyone to stop him, anywhere.
But I can see the darkness,
And I wonder why we don't try one more time?

Now the thief doesn't walk down that road alone.
It seems we all do our best to help him along.
We cry wolf when there are only lambs around.
We say "give me, give me, give me, it's only fair."
The thief only smiles and looks around
At all the greedy people grabbing for their share.
Then the darkness comes, and the thunderclouds roll,
And I can see us headed for a storm.

The thief touches our souls with a dark, evil wand.
He turns love to hate, and steals the heart of man.
The dark clouds will roll, volcanoes will erupt,
Earthquakes will rumble, and tear apart our souls.
We're down to our last moment, the last chance we have.
I pray to God that He'll help us someway.
I feel the strain, sometimes I feel so all alone.
Dear God won't you help us one more time?

I pray that God will help us one more time.

CANDLES

(For a friend's wedding)

(1994)

The flame always burns brighter
When two candles burn together.
The flame is purer and climbs higher
Than one candle on its own.
As time moves onward
The candles grow closer together
And they seem to burn as one.
Their wax runs together,
Flowing from candle to candle
Like arms in a loving embrace,
And becomes tighter as time moves on.
Their flame, burning as one,
Is like a kiss.
The spark of life, of love,
Flowing from one to another.
Finally, as they grow older,
The flame dims, eventually dies.
But the light of the two shines on,
Glowing in God's loving hands.

NAILS

I hold my head in my hands
And I cry, I cry, I cry,
And I slowly dry my eyes.

The tears keep falling and they won't stop.
I hang my head and until I drop.
I feel so much pain and it just won't go away.

Blood dripping down into His eyes,
Scars in His hands from the nails I drive.
I feel the pain but I don't know what to say.

And it's coming, it's coming,
My judgment day.

I feel the pain running deep inside,
Scar in my side that I can't hide.
I turn away every time I see HIS face.

As many times as I've turned away,
A fragile man with feet of clay,
He takes me back with His loving grace.

And it's coming, it's coming,
My judgment day.

And I feel the pain and my shame,
I feel the pain, it's not the same.
And I cry and cry and cry my life away.

Until it all falls down and the pain surrounds,
It clouds my eyes but I survive.
I lift up my hands and pray.

And it's coming, it's coming,
My judgment day.

C.D COLLINS

BLINK OF AN EYE
(1998)

I turned around and went through the door,
I saw the light and looked for more,
But there was nothing there in which I could find her face.
I hurried down the street a ways,
Dreaming of those long past days
But knowing somewhere, somehow, I had lost the race.
I heard a cry deep in the night,
I awoke with terrible fright
And with nowhere to hide I turned and found Your grace.

Your grace, in this place,
No disgrace, in this place, in this place.

They led him to the electric chair
To send him off to who knows where.
Of myself was all I could seem to think.
Nailed to a cross so high,
Weakened so that death was nigh,
And I turned and went off to find myself a drink.
It happens all so hurriedly,
Quicker than the eye can see,
We never knew the whole world was in that blink.

Blink of an eye, blink of an eye,
I can't deny, that blink of an eye, blink of an eye.

What can you say when you see me now,
Struggling through I know not how,
Knowing I wouldn't be here except that He loves me?
I lie, I cheat, I steal, and I lust,
What did I do to earn His trust?
How could one so pure ever love me?
My faults are there for all to see.
Convicted in life's book of history
But still the loving arms will wrap around me.

Wrap around me, wrap around me,
Loving arms will wrap around me, around me.

THE CALL
(1998)

To find another way, I've been running now for days,
Crying out but not heard, never quite understood.
I just can't take it all,
I know I'm bound to fall.

Sooner or later
You have to answer the call,
Running, but not away, praying for just one more day.
Raining down on my head, wondering if I'm alive or dead.

Don't know where to turn,
My poor heart feels the burn,
And sooner or later
I have to answer the call.

Leaving, but not left behind, memories, reflections of my mind.
Searching for the word, where can I be understood?
It's all be said before, you'll soon be knocking at the door.
Which path did you choose, did you answer the call?

I just can't find
Any peace of mind.
Will you play?
Will you choose today.....?

It's all been said before,
Before you're knocking at the door,
Choose your path
And answer the call.

RANTING
(2001)

The mystery of life is confusing,
We all want to know life's plan.
We struggle each day just to learn
Exactly where it is we stand.

Confusion to some is joy to me,
It's the quest for which I yearn.
I am constantly amazed at the things
God has planned for me to learn.

To know it all now, to be content
In my knowledge and my faith,
Would be an end to a spiritual adventure
And for that end, I can wait.

Each day brings despair and hope,
Mixed feelings to figure out.
Each has a special meaning
That's what life is about.

We are here not to know all,
But to learn more with each passing day.
I wouldn't want it any different,
'Cause I think God planned it that way.

GREEN, GREEN HILLS
(1999)

I can testify, with the tears I've cried,
To the pain of separation.
To all the deeds, which have besieged me
And that sent me to the depths of desolation.

All the sleepless nights, my mind churns and fights
The thoughts that can't escape me.
As I toss and turn, the wheels inside still churn,
And it all weighs down on me.

I can remember times, with much simpler rhymes
In the fields where I once roamed.
And if I just knew how, I would go back now
To the green, green hills of home.

And all the people here, all stop and stare
At the one who does not belong here.
In this huddled mass, I don't think I'll last
To survive here one more year.

Life moves all too fast, nothing seems to last,
It's all so superficial.
They all want a part of me, that I don't want to set free,
But they take it against my will.

And in simpler days I remember simpler ways,
We worked our fingers to the bone.
And if I just knew how, I would go back now
To the green, green hills of home.

And I'm crying, and I'm crying
And I'm crying out for You, Lord.
And I need You so, oh please don't let go,
Lead me to the new life Lord, Lord, Lord.

Everything is wrong; I just can't go on,
And I'm crawling back to You.
And I seek Your grace, I seek Your face
In everything I do, Lord.

ALONE
(2000)

Walking down the street, not feeling so fine.
Everyone's talking about a brand new rhyme.
Everybody's moved and I'm standing in place.
I have no clue, I've got egg on my face.

Now who's this God they're all talking about?
Don't think I know but I'd like to find out.
Who's He? Where's He? He's an elusive cat.
I just have to find where He is at.

'Cause my heart is empty, nothing but cheap thrills.
Open it up and out they spill.
'Cause in my life I need something that's real.
Because I'm tired of swallowing this bitter pill.

Alone, I said I'm alone,
Alone and the story goes on.

I used to pray most every day,
But seems God never has anything to say.
I opened my heart to let Him in.
The sign says "Vacant" and He ain't been seen.

Don't know what all this God talk is.
Beginning to think I've been getting the biz.
They say He comes to you in hour of need.
Been needy all my life, Lord come set me free.

'Cause I've been trying to talk to You.
Got a ton of crap I need help through.
But I don't really know quite what to do,
To get my rhyme heard, to get through to You.

I'm dying, crying, trying all the time.
The sounds in my head are a dull street whine.
So God come to me, hear what I've said.
Help me, Lord, because inside I'm dead.

Alone, I said I'm alone.
Alone, does the story go on?

Trying one more time to get through to You.
Won't someone help me, tell me what to do?
If only You could see the shape I'm in.
I'm dying here, Lord, my heartbeat is thin.

Alone, I said I'm alone,
Alone, story ends.

MY HEAVY ARMOR
(2001)

Lord, I'm Tired of wearing this armor
And I'm tired of hefting this sword.
So tired of beating back the demons
That crowd upon my door.

So, Lord, help me to endure now.
Give me strength to carry on.
'Cause this armor's getting heavy
And this sword just feels so wrong.

And I'm so tired of the battle,
My heart is so weary with the pain.
I long for peace and comfort,
To rest at home again.

But the warrior's road is long
And the victories are few,
But I know the final outcome
If I pledge my sword to You.

For we'll all be called to judgment,
And those found righteous may be few,
But I know where I'll stand that day
If I give my life to You.

So, Lord, make my sword hand strong
And my heart pure and bold,
So I may fight on for You
And someday walk Your streets of gold.

GLORY BOUND
(1997)

For far too many years now I've been walking this road
And sometimes I get weary from the load.
It's so hard carrying this load around,
Sometimes it really starts to wear me down.
Then I turn it over to You,
And You will see me through,
Glory bound.

Sometimes right is wrong and wrong is right.
I get lost staring into the starry night.
It's so hard just trying to make it through
All the things that all we people do.
With my eyes straight ahead
I remember the words you said,
Glory Bound.

I know You have the answers that I seek.
I try to hear all the words You speak.
I see You there, wearing that Thorny crown,
And I thank God that I'm Glory bound.

SOMEONE LIKE YOU
(1998)

Tell me it's true, it ain't no lie.
I need Your love, to help me get by.
I see the light, shining on me.
It caresses my soul, helps me to see.

And I've been searching all of my life,
For someone like You.
And I've been searching all of my life,
For someone like You.

Deep in the night, down in my heart,
There's a light that shines, a heavenly spark.
I believe in You, because You believed in me.
You saved my soul, at Calvary.

And I've been searching all of my life,
For someone like You.
And I've been searching all of my life,
For someone like You.

When I was down, You were there.
You wrapped Your arms around my soul.
You picked me up, out of despair,
Changed my life and made me whole.

And I'm so glad that in my Life,
I've someone like You.
And I'm so glad that in my Life,
I've someone like You.

ALL I KNOW

(1994)

Can You hear me, can You feel me, can You read my thoughts?
Can You see me, can You heal me, can You see me through
All the hard times, all the low times, all the pain I bear?
Can You hear me, can You heal me, will You be there?

Now I know that Your word is true.
Now I know I'm so in love with You.
Now I know that love is real,
Now I know You feel just what I feel.
That's all I know.

Will I hear You, will I feel You, will Your thoughts be mine?
Will I know You, let You live through this heart of mine?
Will I stand strong, not be headstrong, will I let them see?
All the love there, the life that we share, will they see You in me?

Now I know that Your word is true.
Now I know I'm so in love with You.
Now I know that love is real,
Now I know You feel just what I feel.
That's all I know.

I've been so wrong it seems for so long, can I make it right?
All the pain's gone, all the hurt's gone, You helped me through the night.
I received Your grace, I seek Your face, Your will be mine.
I will seek You, I will follow You, until the end of time.

4 STATE OF THINGS

Sometimes there are happenings in life that really shake you to your very core. The world seems out of alignment with the Cosmos, and things are off kilter. I feel like that often. We let political differences and ideology change what we really are. We get so obsessed with happenings in the world and ideologies that we forget the important things.

Maybe I am just speaking for myself. However, I cannot help but feel that others are often mystified by the happenings as well. There is no compromise in the political world, and so nothing is accomplished. It is sad to me that we strive to be more like what we think others want us to be, rather than what we should be.

Love, family, God, compassion, and charity should be things we focus on.

FAITH: SHAKEN, NOT STIRRED
(2000)

Faith can be such a flimsy thing,
Whimsical at times, sometimes strong,
But it moves and never seems to rest.
There are events that test our faith,
And even faith built over a long life
Can be shaken when put to the test.

A man, so proud, so strong, and full of life
Striving to be righteous and straight,
Full of faith and somewhat headstrong.
War hero, sports hero, patriarch of his line,
Wisdom, his to disperse to willing, young minds.
But where and to whom does faith belong?

Our faith in heroes, our faith in God,
Surely this is faith well placed.
Can any faith be true in this God forsaken place?
Lifeblood washed down an old storm drain
Mingling with sewage and sludge.
Is this where faith leads us at the end of the race?

I picked his spectacles up from off the ground
Where they had fallen at the shot,
Covered in blood and particles of brain.
Not much to show for a life
Full of pride and hope and truth,
That I was slowly washing down the drain.

His blood on my hands, his blood on my arms,
Covered in blood to my knees
And still there was more to be washed away.
Down the drive, down the walk,
Slowly swirling down the drain.
There was no place to hide that day.

A PICTURE OF ME

How could a man, so strong in truth,
Always overcoming and defeating the trials,
Choose an ending like this?
No fair-thee-wells or long good-byes,
No loving hugs or embraces,
No last goodbye sealed with a kiss.

A shot, a mere blink of an eye,
A second frozen in time
Wipes out all that he did before.
No grieving family attending bedside,
Just a shot in time.
I am left to clean up the gore.

Is this what life is? Is this what life is for?
Living a long, good life,
Only to have life's final door
Slammed in your face
Like some unwanted salesman?
I am left scrubbing the floor.

The blood, now like iodine,
Soaked hard and fast into my skin.
The blood of my dearest kin
Will always be there,
No matter how hard I scrub.
I will always bear part of his sin.

So tell me God, all knowing and wise,
What do I say when I look into the eyes
That stare back from the mirror I see?
Do I still have faith
Like him that went before,
Or did faith die with the blood that's upon me?

OH! IRELAND
(1991)

Oh! Ireland, Oh! Ireland,
I never walked your castle walls,
Never strolled your rolling hills,
Never heard your sad pipe call.

But I have dreamed always
Of walking across your lands,
Of sinking my toes into your soil,
Awakening a new man.

I hear the poetry of your people,
That proud, romantic race.
And were I but there
I'd kiss every blessed face.

Oh! Ireland, Oh! Ireland,
I may never see your green hills,
But you will be in my heart always,
You're ever a part of me, if it's God's will.

THE STORM
(1989)

Lightning flashes,
The wind roars.
Thunder clashes and tears down the doors.
The evil lurks within us
Trying to be free.
We deny its existence,
We just can't see.

Rivers rage,
Run out of control.
The waters rise and flood our souls.
But we go on living
And I don't know why.
Life is so unforgiving,
We live to die.

Mothers weep,
The children die.
Lifeblood drained, I wonder why.
We just go on killing,
Can't we see what we do?
If we are so willing
It will kill us too.

LONELY OLD MEN
(1987)

Lonely old men, sitting down by the beach,
Waiting for their ship to come in.
Lonely old men, with their life out of reach,
Wishing that they were young again.

Sad, sad faces, down by the shore,
Waiting for life to end.
Faces that never reached out to open the door,
And let the flood of life in.

I don't know which way the tide flows,
Life slips out far from the shore.
And the lonely old men, are wishing again,
That they were young once more.

Pretty young girls, in a crowded shopping mall,
Just trying to catch young men's eyes.
Lonely young boys, stand so straight and so tall,
Answer not with words, but just sighs.

Lonely young man living life on the street,
Just doing what he can to get by.
Receiving so much resistance from the people he meets,
When he's only trying to survive.

I don't know which way the tide flows,
Life slips out far from the shore.
And the lonely old men, are wishing again,
That they were young once more.

There are no smiles, on the faces I see,
We've learned not to let others in.
But I do see our waste as it flows to the sea,
And no one can say where it will end.

And it's really so hard, but I don't know why,
Our innocence fades everyday.
But we just sit and wait for our worlds to collide,
I guess that's just the price that we pay.

We turn our backs on our brothers these days,
Not caring what they have to say.
Life slips from our hands, out far from the shore,
And I'm just wishing I was young once more.

Life slips from our hands, out far from the shore,
And I'm just wishing I was young once more.

Note: This is song from a play I wrote of the same name, which will soon be published

DESOLATION
(2001)

Escape the desolation, run away from here
To find warmth and comfort, the way is not always clear.
Leave this all behind me and try to get away.
It's not always easy, some of me remains behind.
Deep in my heart, there is a fire growing strong,
It tells me all is not right, and that everything can't be wrong.
I find consolation, when I lie in your arms.
Take away the bitter feeling, chase away the biting cold.

To lie in your arms, Love, to fly way with you from here,
To escape my own cruel prison, holding you close, so dear.
To leave my world behind, to escape to yours with you,
My heart's perfect vision, and a love I know is true.
Can't remember where I've been
And I don't know just where I'm bound,
But I just hope and pray, every day
That I might find my peace in your arms.

Escape of the struggle that is the life I've known,
The brilliant fires of nighttime, and the cold ash that washes the day.
Seek peace and solace, in a place so far from here
That the sounds of the terror can't reach me to build my fear.
So hold me close and protect me, from all that I fear.
Hold me close, till my days all turns clear.
To hide in your arms, Love, my refuge in the storm
When it's raining all around me, with you I'll always be warm.

To lie in your arms, Love, to fly away with you from here,
To escape my own cruel prison, lying in your arms so dear
To leave my world behind, to escape to yours with you,
My heart's perfect vision, and a love I know is true.

And In your arms I hide, to you only I confide,
And seek the peace and comfort I've never known.
You pluck me up from Hell, Love, and make me whole again.
When I lie in your arms, Love, I begin to love again.

Torments of my youth, slowly begin to fade away,
And on the new horizon, I see a brand new day.
Hatred rolls away, as new life creeps in.
And I can feel the passion begin to rise in me again.
It makes life new, as if I was born today.
I lie in your arms and there I always want to stay,
Hold me close and love me, don't ever let me go.
I cry to the heavens, for the one that loves me so.

To lie in your arms, Love, to fly way with you from here,
To escape my own cruel prison, lying in your arms so dear.
To leave my world behind, to escape to yours with you,
My heart's perfect vision, and a love I know is true.
Can't remember just where I've been,
And I don't know just where I'm bound,
But I just hope and pray, every day
I might find my peace in your arms.

FIRE

I feel the breath of burning desire,
I feel the flames growing higher and higher.
I feel the heat of desire and passion.
What does it feel like, you keep asking?

Feels like fire
Feels like fire
Feels like fire

Passion runs deep, I can't hide.
Can't see the light, I'm mystified.
Burning and churning, where do I turn?
Stick around now and watch me burn.

Burn like fire
Burn like fire
Burn like fire

NIGHTFALL
(1998)

Another night, another night falls.
Another day slowly dies.
Will that day not live again,
Or will it be born anew with the sunrise?

Another night, another night falls,
And the flowers bow their heads.
Will they wilt and perish forever,
Or will they bloom on the 'morrow instead?

Another night, another night falls.
A star shoots across the sky.
Will my wishes remain unheard,
Or will God hear my cry?

Another night, another night falls
On the wretch called mankind.
But with the new tomorrow,
Maybe a glimmer of hope in our minds.

Another night, another night falls.

THE HANGOVER BLUES
(2002)

To each their own
And to own their each,
Their souls their own to sell.
I'm so tired of living in a place so much like Hell.
Spit in your eye
In a pig's sty,
A world so very unclean.
Don't you wish that sometimes you could know exactly it means?

One in the hand,
Two in the bush,
Fifteen all bound and gagged,
It's so sad to live and die, not knowing what we had.
Stomach turns,
A fire that burns
A night seemingly without end.
Hangover blues were what I knew, riding a drunken binge.

Windswept streets,
Monkey beat
Organ grinder on the dole,
And you with your monkey shines warring for my soul.
Teary eyed,
Wonder why
We always question what we know?
Salvation's gate we undertake but fight hard not to go.

Sailor's moon,
Cow and the spoon,
The knife ran away with the girl.
I should have fought harder to not let them take her from my world.
Chapter and verse,
Horse drawn hearse,
Soon to be knocking on Hell's door.
Sorry to have lived and died, just working as life's whore.

Pearly gates,
So irate,
That I could be knocking down.
Glad that I didn't end up lost but that somehow I was found.
Dead man's eyes,
So unwise
To pour these thoughts out on you.
But I guess that is what happens when you have the hangover blues.

OUT OF THE MIST
(2000)

I came out of the mist.
Dreary day, long face,
Looking for warmth,
Shelter from the cold.
Through the rain I saw
A wee cottage painted green
And it was shelter there I sought.

Inside, lit by fire,
Bright faces, warm hearts,
I had a pint, then another.
Conversations by fireside,
Jokes at the bar,
I no longer felt weary
Though I had traveled so far.

Ecstasy on my palette,
Flavors to caress,
Warm my soul and belly,
Good food, good friends.
And Guinness never ending
Found in the emerald cottage
Just this side of the mist.

THE LAST PLACE GOD MADE

Rain falling down upon my face.
Heat rising in this disturbing place.
I can't seem to find any peace of mind,
Standing in the shade
In the last place God made.

Growing old but not gracefully.
Living in the past, wondering where I'll be.
Not knowing why I can't decide,
On the hand to play
In the last place God made.

Now sounds of silence surround me.
It's so loud I can hardly see.
I can't live for today,
It's not for me
In the last place God made.

HEAT OF THE NIGHT
((1987)

You feel the sweat pouring,
You start to feel so strange.
Then your palms start itching,
Man, you never felt this way.
Then you turn towards her
In the back seat of your car.
You say you never thought
Things would ever go this far.

In the heat of the night
You feel good holding her tight.
Everything feels all right
In the heat of the night.

You stop outside a convenience store
And look in through the door.
You say you plan to stop this
After one last big score.
You never thought you'd stoop so low
To making money in this way.
Didn't someone tell you, son
That crime just don't pay?

It's the heat of the night.
The damp dark test without light.
You just can't get up out of the fight
It's the heat of the night.

You feel the harsh rain come down,
It stings you like a knife.
Hot sweltering summer heat,
The hottest in your life.
You pass two lovers in a car,
You hear the sirens wail.
Some punk at a convenience store
Blew the owner straight to Hell.

It's the heat of the night.
The whole world's on fire tonight.
Scream out loud it's all right,
It's the heat of the night.

INNOCENCE
(1989)

Rivers run cold
Harsh is the land,
Without hope of change.
We're in a world where fear
Is master of our souls.

Uncleansed water boils,
Purity slips away
Into the belly of the beast,
Into a time whose hands
Move too fast.

The beast rises,
Demands payments
Of innocence and youth
And strips away
The sparkle from our eyes.

Youth is gone.
Our innocence slips away
Into the night,
Into the belly of the beast
Where rivers run cold.

5 A POLITICAL WORLD

This is what our world has become, a political world. We are not individuals anymore; it seems we must align ourselves with a certain group. I choose to rebel.

WINDS OF CONFUSION
(1991)

The wind of pain blows through my head,
Roars so loud I can't hear what's been said.
The chips are down, the battle line has been drawn.
Oh! Please tell me what went wrong.
Winds of confusion, blowing through my mind,
Winds of confusion get me every time.

Scorching sand lies beneath my feet.
My skin is burned and I can't stand the heat.
The shifting sand reflects changing times.
All that hate really infects my mind.
Winds of confusion, blowing through my head,
Winds of confusion, it's the land of the dead.

Warplanes are rushing over the sand.
Missiles of death are at our command.
Psychotic ruler cries out in rage.
I want out of this story, please turn the page.
Winds of confusion, can't you hear what they say?
Winds of confusion blow me away.

A CHANGE MAY COME

(2000)

Being the type of man I am, quick to temper and to forgive,
Out of sorts with government and friends, tired of the life I live,
I often wonder what would be, could be, if only I could make a change?
But alas, nothing changes, it remains the same,
And will for the rest of my days.

But if people would just listen, to the song of rebellion in the air;
If only we would hearken to the rebel's call, act and not despair,
A change might finally come, on the wispy wind of the night,
But changes seldom come, when no one cares enough to fight.

Only if one truly cares, for the outcome more than self,
Only if the goal is noble, the soldier bold, not blind nor deaf,
With the goal in sight and battle cry heard, the soldier can succeed.
When that cause is noble, perhaps a change we'll see indeed.

SWILL
1990

Rivers run down to the sea,
Like blood flowing through our arteries.
Once they carried soil and life,
Now they're full of the disease of strife.
Discarded remnants of our world
Flow to the sea in a dirty swirl.

We smother ourselves in a sea of trash,
Washed from mountains of landfill hash.
Higher and higher they seem to climb
While sounds of our machinery whine.
We build higher and dig deeper but all the while
We grow harder and colder, forget to smile.

Knowledge and culture lost in a cloud
Of drugs and smoke screaming aloud
"Buy me, use me, I'm your friend,"
Only to leave you dying in the end.
Needle stuck in a young girl's arm,
But still we fail to heed the alarm.

That hits like a hammer striking a rail,
But strikes hollow like a rusty nail.
Fastening the top to a long pine box,
A coffin for humanity cursed by a pox.
Coffin thrown on a mountain landfill,
Then washed to the sea in a dirty swill.

WALKING MAN

Walking man, roadside weary,
Rain soaked coat heavy.
Morning mist like tears from sad mothers' eyes.
Crying, dead by red hand.
Black beret washed down storm gutter,
Cleansing the weary Derry street.

Another time, another face,
Everything not in its place.
Walking man so very tired, so weary,
Struggles to comprehend.
Dying young, dying old, all dying,
Derry Street dead.

Walking man, tired and wet,
Cold mist bites face and hand.
Crying sky cries for all but for no one.
Dead, not seen but somehow heard,
Rankles, haunts, does not end.

PICTURE OF ME
(1988)

I saw a picture of you from 1916.
There was fire in your eyes, you were barely nineteen.
There was pain on your face from the things you had seen.
When I look at you I see a picture of me.

The next time I saw you it was 1921.
Your face had aged but you were still young.
You had chased the British across the Irish Sea
But when I look at you I see a picture of me.

And oh, where does the time go?
What lies ahead now for me?
I pray for somebody to please tell me why,
When I look at a picture of you I see a picture of me.

I found a photograph of the beach at Normandy.
You had aged a lot, that I could see.
There was still the fire from a young man's eyes,
But when I looked closer I realized it was a picture of me.

I open the chest in the attic on a whim,
I saw your pictures from Korea and Viet Nam.
A chest full of medals, body half blown away,
But no, could it really be a picture of me?

And now I know they were all pictures of me,
Going to face battle, brave the artillery.
I'm all the young men we've sent off to war.
When you look at them you'll see a picture of me.

And oh, where does the time go?
What lies ahead now for me?
I pray for somebody to please tell me why,
When I look at a picture of you I see a picture of me.

SUMMER RAIN
(1987)

Thunder rumbles, as the clouds roll,
Soft summer rain falls from the sky,
Onto the fields where the rain
Washes scars from the land.
If only that summer rain
Could wash the scars from my back
And the pain from my mind.

I remember warm summer days.
We walked the fields where children played.
We shared hopes and dreams, carried out schemes
Until the day turned into night.
If only that summer rain
Could wash the scars from my back
And the pain from my mind.

Nights are long and nights are hard,
But we'll carry our crosses and bear our chains.
Until a new day dawns
And the long night fades into the mist.
If only that summer rain
Could wash the scars from my back
And the pain from my mind.

CAMELOT
(1989)

Camelot is gone,
And his dreams are unfulfilled.
We're still struggling with the same questions
That we were when he was killed.
I don't know how we wandered
From the plans laid out that day,
It seemed that men were made of granite,
When we were only made of clay.

Camelot is gone.
The sunshine has gone from the day.
We still have more questions than answers,
And we've not quite found the way.
We land men on the moon,
Conquer the depths of the sea,
But still we have not found a way
For man to live in harmony.

Camelot is gone,
It may never be again.
Unless we learn from our mistakes,
Quit committing the same old sins.
We could live together as one,
In a land that is truly free,
But until we learn and live the answers,
Camelot can never be.

PRAYER TO MOTHERS OF THE DAMNED
(1988)

Mother, Mother, hear my plea.
I feel that everyone has forsaken me.
I was carried away in the gloom of the night,
For a cause that can't be won, but still I had to fight.

Here in Long Kesh prison, I sit in my cell.
Listening to the sounds of poor souls as they wail.
Crying out for justice, or just to be heard,
But there is no help, no encouraging word.

Darkness clouds our minds with visions of hate
And memories of comrades we cannot forsake.
We have no sunlight, no fresh water from cold wells.
We sit in Dante's dungeon, a place that's a living hell.

The dampness eats away at the edges of our souls.
I shiver from the hopelessness, not the terrible cold.
Freedom is a concept I no longer comprehend,
I see only my mind's corner, but not around the bend.

I see visions of a tunnel, with a light at the end.
Hot as the fires of hell, bright as only God could send.
I reach out to touch it, but it drifts way,
Then I'm back in my cell, chalking up one more day.

You are surely mother's of the damned, for its damned we are.
Your memory seems so close, but your touch seems so far.
Light a candle for me, at Mass when you can,
And pray for my poor soul, be it of beast or man.

SHADOWS

(1987)

Children's voices out in the street,
Nightfall comes and you hear them retreat,
To the shadows, the shadows of our hearts,
To the shadows, the shadows that tear us apart.

Screams in their eyes, a song in their soul,
I recognize the pain their song holds.
It's an old song, sung in a different key,
It's the same song that was sung by you and me.

Where do the children go in the night?
Where do the shadows go when there's no light?
Why have some given up the fight?
We can justify it, but that don't make it right.

Broken mirror out in the street
Reflects the shattered lives of the people we meet
On Falls Road, or any city street.
On Falls Road, it could be any city street.

When will it end, why can't we stop
Trying to pretend we are something we're not?
It's an old game, but now it' time for an end.
It's an old game, but one we'd better win.

Where do the children go in the night?
Where do the shadows go when there's no light?
Why have some given up the fight?
We can justify it, but that don't make it right.

SKY

(1988)

We live our lives on the razor's edge,
Living one day to the next.
Day by day, hour by hour,
Never looking back
At the mistakes we made,
Lives with which we paid.
I wonder why?
Maybe someday
We'll all fly away
To the sky.

We put violent death beneath the ground
To fly at our command.
We scatter our waste all around,
We can no longer walk in the sand.
The air we breathe is full of disease,
Products of mankind.
Mighty rain forests, brought to their knees,
It seems we've really lost our minds.
Maybe we'll see
The way that it can be if we try.
Maybe someday
We'll all fly away
To the sky.

www.ingramcontent.com/pod-product-compliance
Lightning Source LLC
Chambersburg PA
CBHW031324040426
42443CB00005B/206